BOOK ANALYSIS

Written by Natacha Cerf and Alice Rasson
Translated by Ciaran Traynor

AF143855

Promise at Dawn
BY ROMAIN GARY

Bright
≡Summaries.com

ROMAIN GARY 1

French novelist

PROMISE AT DAWN 2

A son's debt to his mother

SUMMARY 3

A mother's devotion
A time of war

CHARACTER STUDY 7

Romain Gary
Mina Owczynska

ANALYSIS 11

Maternal love
The power of imagination
The importance and role of humour
An epic novel
The idealisation of France

FURTHER REFLECTION 22

Some questions to think about...

FURTHER READING 24

ROMAIN GARY

FRENCH NOVELIST

- **Born in Lithuania in 1914.**
- **Died in Paris in 1980.**
- **Notable works:**
  - *The Roots of Heaven* (1956), novel
  - *The Life Before Us* (1975), novel
  - *The Kites* (1980), novel

Romain Gary (born Romain Kacew, and also known by the pseudonym Émile Ajar) was a Jewish-French novelist who was born in Lithuania in 1914. He came to France when he was 14 years old. After graduating with a degree in law, he fought in the Free French Forces until the end of the Second World War (1939-1945). He then pursued a diplomatic career until 1960. He committed suicide in Paris in 1980.

Romain Gary is the only French writer to have received the Prix Goncourt on two separate occasions: once for his novel *The Roots of Heaven*, published under the name Gary, and once for *The Life Before Us*, published under the pseudonym Ajar. Gary is particularly known for this choice to conceal his name.

PROMISE AT DAWN

A SON'S DEBT TO HIS MOTHER

- **Genre**: autobiographical novel
- **Reference edition**: Gary, R. (1988) *Promise at Dawn*. Trans. Beach, J. M. Brussels: New Directions.
- **1st edition**: 1961 (French edition first published in 1960)
- **Themes**: maternal love, war, death, promise, sickness, irony

Promise at Dawn is an autobiographical novel first published in 1960. It tells the story of Gary's past, not as he actually experienced it but how he views it retrospectively in light of who he has become.

Gary spent his youth trying to live up to his mother Mina's artistic expectations for him. After his mother's business went bankrupt, the two left Poland for Nice, where they achieved financial security thanks to the hotel and boarding house that Mina managed. Romain graduated with a degree in law and then joined the Free French Air Forces. He returned to Nice in 1945, high on the success of his novella *A European Education* and his title of *Compagnon de la Libération* ("Companion of the Liberation"), to discover that his mother had died: the letters that he had been receiving from her had been written in advance.

SUMMARY

A MOTHER'S DEVOTION

Among the tales and stories which came from Romain's mother's imagination is one about three gods, who Romain has to fight. As a child, he knew that his mother wanted him to defy Totoche, the god of Stupidity, Merzavka, the god of Absolute Truth and Total Righteousness, and Filoche, the god of Mediocrity, Prejudice and Hatred. For Mina and her son, they are the symbolic representations of humanity's worst vices.

A strong, courageous woman, Mina works incredibly hard to provide for her son alone, as she is divorced. The little boy is overwhelmed with love for his mother and wants to do something for her. The future writer believes in a mysterious force which will lead him to shower her with his successes to compensate for her life of sacrifice and self-denial.

They leave Moscow for Wilno (today known as Vilnius) where Mina fights tooth and nail so the two can lead a comfortable life. Thanks to her hat business, they are relatively well-off for a time. Unfortunately, Romain falls ill, and the resulting medical fees ruin them. His mother's business, *Maison nouvelle, Grand Salon de Haute Couture de Paris*, is declared bankrupt. They then leave Wilno for Warsaw, where they struggle to get by. Romain begins to go to a Polish school.

One day, one of Romain's classmates insults his mother, but he says nothing. Mina forbids him to ever set foot in the school again, furious that he did not defend her honour.

Later on, she goes to the French consulate so that they can become French residents. In Nice, Mina sells a block of flats, which are then given to her to manage. One part is transformed into a hotel and restaurant. The customers come from all over the world.

Romain leaves Nice in 1933 to continue his studies at the law faculty of Aix-Marseille University. He feels extremely emasculated: having to live off his mother, now an old, ragged woman, gnaws away at him.

In Paris, where he goes to continue his studies, his novel *L'Orage* ("The Storm") is published in the weekly newspaper *Gringoire*. He graduates and comes to the end of his military training.

A TIME OF WAR

France joins the war in 1940. Romain is the only one of the 300 graduates to be promoted not to the rank of officer, but to the rank of corporal. Unfortunately, the fact that he has been a French citizen for a relatively short amount of time is viewed with suspicion. Filoche, disguised as a pilot, has already spread his prejudices to Avord Flying School. In Bordeaux-Mérignac, Romain spends six hours a day in the air as a flight instructor. He soon becomes a sergeant. At this time, he receives a telegram informing him of his mother's very worrying state of health. He is wracked with the anguish of not being able to honour her with his achievements:

> "The idea that she might die before I had done all that she expected of me, that she might leave this world without ever having known *justice*, that projection in the heavens of a human system of weights and measures, seemed to me to be a denial of the most elementary common sense, of good manners and law, and to show a sort of gangsterlike attitude on the part of fate that justified one in calling the police, invoking the moral code and the intervention of some supreme legal authority."

Nevertheless, he continues to receive letters from her, which reassures him. He does not think for a second that she had actually written all of them before dying. He does not find out until three years later.

The armistice is signed in June 1940, but Romain wants to continue the fight. He is extremely proud to be a naturalised French citizen, and sings the praises of France to all who care to listen to him. He therefore goes to Morocco, where resistance efforts are said to continue. However, when he arrives, he discovers that the North African authorities have already accepted the armistice. General de Gaulle's (French statesman, 1890-1970) call on 18 June 1940 to continue the fight has clearly not been heard.

Romain leaves Africa on board a British cargo ship transporting a contingent of Polish soldiers. He arrives in Glasgow and is given several missions. He then heads back to Africa. While on board the *Arundel Castle*, Roman begins to write novellas again, imagining that his mother is still by his side.

In Africa, he does not have the chance to be a hero:

> "I don't think that during those five years of war, half of the time with my squadron, broken up only by periods spent in the hospital, I accomplished more than four or five combat missions, which I remember today with the vague feeling of being a good son."[1]

Just after being made sub-lieutenant, he contracts typhoid fever. However, fuelled by his mother's vitality which courses through his veins, he recovers.

His novella *A European Education*, written at night at the Hartford Bridge airbase, is published by an English company. Gary is pleased for his mother:

> "I had become neither a hero nor an Ambassador of France, not even a First Secretary, but all the same I was beginning to keep my promise and to give some meaning to her struggles and her sacrifices. Slim and slight though my little book might be, it seemed to me to weigh heavily on the scales."

After a particularly rough mission, he receives the Cross of the Liberation from Charles de Gaulle himself. When the Liberation finally comes, Romain returns to the Hôtel-Pension Mermonts to learn that his mother died three and a half years ago. She had seen to it that the 250 letters that she had written before dying would be delivered to her son regularly, in order to support him.

---

1. This quotation has been translated by BrightSummaries.com.

CHARACTER STUDY

Romain Gary is sensitive and turns sources of indignation into his inspiration. His autobiographical story is written with tears and anger. He and his mother are often victims of human stupidity and nastiness, but he always has the willpower to pull through and escape the anti-Semitic threats which loom from all angles. Literature is his weapon. He therefore revolts against injustice through his writing. In other words, writing for him is a way to assuage his thirst for justice.

Gary is an idealist: he revolts against injustice and the cruelty and stupidity of men, but does not despair about human nature: he claims he is a "star eater". *Promise at Dawn* is undeniably a song of hope. The central theme of the novel is the realisation of an ideal which is fostered in him from an early age: Gary hungers for the absolute from the cradle to the grave.

He begins his story with an affectionate description of daydreaming on the beach at Big Sur (California), where he is surrounded by the benevolence of the wild coast. This is the revelation of an essential affection in his eyes: nature. In addition, in almost every chapter he describes a tender scene with his mother. Of course, the story also has many instances of embarrassment and shame caused by his mother's theatricality and over-the-top nature, but he always prefers to endure being ridiculed rather than make his mother think he is rejecting her. Emotion is at the heart of the tale.

"My mother was Jewish. But that didn't matter. What mattered was expression. Who cares what language it was said in?"[2] This is how she blesses him before he goes off to war. These words demonstrate that he cares little about belonging to a certain community or social, cultural or religious sphere. He rejects labels and refuses to be defined according to any determiners or traditions. Family and country of origin are perceived as obstacles to sweep aside in order to realise his dream. He does not allow roles to be imposed upon him from the outside and makes the choice of freedom. In this way, he frees himself from his roots: he writes in French and sometimes in English, but never in Russian or Polish. Gary prefers everywhere else to his origins; he is defined by permanent movement. He has a dynamic, resourceful personality, a thirst for action and a huge amount of willpower. He is a picaro, a character without scruples who rises from the common people to join the ranks of the elite thanks to their wits and skill.

He is also childish, naïve and impulsive, and this side of his personality is maintained by his exclusive link of love with his mother. This is the driving force of his combat for justice: he has to correct the world in the name of harmony and the beauty of good stories. This fight is possible thanks to his naivety. Love, tenderness and courage are the most important things in the life of this solitary, misunderstood writer.

---

2. This quotation has been translated by BrightSummaries.com.

MINA OWCZYNSKA

Mina Owczynska is Romain's mother. She is divorced and raises her son by herself. She is Jewish and is forced to flee anti-Semitic Russia and Poland, and gives everything she has to guarantee her son a bright future. Working several jobs at once and sometimes making sacrifices in order to feed her son, Mina is the emblematic figure of courage. She is extremely determined and uses her intelligence and wits to reach her goals. However, Mina Owczynska is also an exceptionally sensitive woman: she often bursts into tears, using this action to give meaning to what she does. She has an extreme, passionate nature.

Romain's mother never complains, in spite of the terrible situations she and her son are forced to endure. She tells her son beautiful stories, which help them to carry on. She tries to reinvent reality with her imagination and in this way expresses a confidence in existence which she wishes to pass on to her child. Mina creates an idealised vision of France, which offers the possibility of a life without persecution:

> "The land of France, which, from my earliest childhood, my mother conjured up for me in her lyrical and inspired descriptions, has become for me a fairy tale, a mythical place, a poetical masterpiece that no fact of life, no contact with reality could ever encompass or reveal."

This legend turns out to be partially true, since it is in France that Romain realises his ambitions and experiences fraternity (a French jeweller decides to put his confidence in them and give them money, the waiter at the Capoulade lets Romain eat croissants for free, and so on). Mina has therefore taught her son that dreams can become reality if we just make the effort to realise them.

ANALYSIS

Romain is gifted with his mother's passionate and uncondi-tional love from the moment he is born:

> "In your mother's love, life makes you a promise at the dawn of life that it will never keep. After that first encounter so early in the dawn, each time a woman takes you in her arms and presses you to her heart and murmurs sweet words into your ear, you will always do your best to forget and to believe, but you will always know better. You will always crawl back to your mother's grave and howl like a lost dog."

In return, the author wants to make his mother's dreams come true. The entire book highlights how he accomplishes his mother's wishes for his success (you will be an ambas-sador, a great writer, and so on). The reader could even be tempted to think that Gary invented some of his mother's aspirations to show that he achieved all of them.

The novel is completely built around a positive image of maternal love. However, Gary does not shy away from describing his mother's extravagant nature, which some-times makes him the butt of jokes, but the vital energy she breathes into him outweighs these faults. *Promise at Dawn* is both an homage and a declaration of love to his mother, who he is completely devoted to. The autobiographical tale never criticises her. Mina's overbearing and overprotective nature are seen as a way to improve her son. She is always there, even beyond death, and has made him into the man he has become. In a way, it is his mother's blind love which allows them to pull through such a hostile time in history. The possessive, all-consuming relationship the two share, which sometimes even becomes destructive, is key here. This all-consuming nature can also be seen in *Promise at Dawn* with the frequent replacement of "I" by "we": "And so, with music, dancing and painting out of the way, we resigned ourselves to literature, in spite of the venereal peril." Romain and Mina's dreams morph into one. Their desires, carried by the strength of the link which unites them, thereby become possible.

Gary knows that her mother's diabetes will eventually kill her. Separated from her by the war, he internalises her: she begins to live inside him by sheer force of imagination. The author constructs her image in an increasingly lyrical and emotional manner the more he realises that their separation will turn out to be permanent. Their conversations alternate with war tales, and Mina gradually takes on mythical dimensions. She remains at the centre of the action: the narrator's "I" always comes after the reactions of the inner character who lives inside him. She is a physical, imperious and dominating presence who represents justice and just words:

> "My mother was outraged. She didn't allow me a moment's peace. She would become angry, fly into a rage, and protest. I couldn't calm her down. She would blaze up in every drop of my blood [...] she was scandalised, deeply wounded by North Africa's refusal to answer her call."[3]

---

3. This quotation has been translated by BrightSummaries.com.

Gary describes her with an abundance of realistic details to make her presence even more tangible:

> "She followed me everywhere, brandishing her stick, and I could see her face clearly, now imploring and indignant, now with that expression of incomprehension which I knew so well. She was still wearing her gray cloak, her gray and violet hat and a string of pearls around her neck."

The exalted presence of his mother, reincarnated inside his body, makes Romain keep his promise: he cannot fail when she is watching. Loyalty and the love which binds them encourage him and give him the strength to face the future. His mother's words have a prophetic strength, as we see from the symbolic episode of Mina's letters, which are sent regularly to her son after she dies until the end of the war. Although this episode is probably not entirely true, it gives a certain physical presence to the voice from beyond the grave. Her missives reflect what she expects from him and encourage him to live up to her expectations. Through this noble form of trickery – Gary's memories on the one hand, his mother's letters on the other – they continue to communicate after death, which illustrates the overwhelming power of love:

> "I invented things around me with all the love and loyalty I was capable of [...] Leaning over the waves, I drew experiences from my past with both hands: snippets of exchanged sentences, words I had heard a thousand times, attitudes and gestures which I had never forgotten, the essential themes which flowed through my life like threads of light which she

wove herself and which she had never let go of."[4]

THE POWER OF IMAGINATION

Romain has an overactive imagination, just like his mother. This characteristic governs the two characters' daily lives, as they are constantly immersed in their imaginations. This aspect of the novel gives it a very theatrical quality. Moreover, the borders between reality and fiction are blurred on many occasions.

This quality that the two characters share has several functions, which gives it a certain power. Firstly, it gives them the strength to pursue their goals. This is particularly the case when Romain imagines his mother encouraging him, talking with him and motivating him throughout the war. This mental creativity continues to give his fight meaning.

Moreover, imagination allows the characters to make their reality less insipid and to give them the feeling that their actions are not in vain. When he is still a child, Romain sees a huge arena in a pile of bricks in the yard of their building, and imagines himself accomplishing his first feats as a gladiator. His mother, for her part, naïvely attributes every great military achievement she reads about in the newspaper to her heroic son. She reinvents reality with her imagination in order to make herself and others see her and her son in a better light. Imagination can therefore be used to reconfigure reality and give it more flavour and meaning.

---

4. This quotation has been translated by BrightSummaries.com.

Finally, this power of imagination reaches its peak in the passages where the characters literally lie about reality. One comic episode which illustrates this is Romain's mother's deception when she presents her clients with the supposed Monsieur Paul Poiret, a famous figure in the Parisian haute couture scene, who is actually none other than one of her actor friends in disguise.

This ambiguity in the distinction between reality and fiction is illustrated in certain passages of the novel, where literary and narrative terminology is used to describe real life. When he finds out that he will not be an officer, Romain states: "I remained true to the character I had chosen to play." Moreover, he says he "regard[s] life as an artistic medium" and compares it to a literary genre.

THE IMPORTANCE AND ROLE OF HUMOUR

The author uses a great deal of humour within the text in a variety of forms for different ends:

- **Irreverence in the search for authenticity and humanity**. Gary is intentionally satirical and cynical about certain ideas, values and positions in order to denounce appearances and find authenticity again. The characters in *Promise at Dawn* demonstrate this: in particular, the author's mother scorns the codes and social norms of the elite. For example, she does not hesitate to ask the King of Sweden to right the wrong done to her son after he is refused membership of a private tennis club.
- **Ridicule to defend his values at the expense of all rea-**

lism. Gary considers himself to be a poetic clown. In the book, there is a combination of a sort of naïve lyricism, in order to give him the best chance of achieving his ideals, and derision before the powerlessness of his conviction to change the world. Gary is a modern-day Don Quixote (the hero of the book of the same name by Miguel de Cervantes, Spanish writer, 1547-1616): an idealist whose perseverance makes him slightly ridiculous.

- **Derision to tackle anxiety**. Humour is also a way for Gary to learn to accept himself by forgetting, to a certain extent, his image and the weight of the roles that he gives himself. For him, self-mockery is a survival instinct: haunted by the fear of failure, he uses it to alleviate his anxiety. Making light of a situation is already a form of resistance. Humour helps him to bear and face up to anxiety without denying it: it diffuses difficult situations where seriousness would only paralyse them. *Promise at Dawn* also contains many dramatic situations, which are all overcome with laughter. This is the case with the tragic scene where a soldier who committed suicide is buried by his comrades with heavy hearts. Tragedy turns to farce when they realise that they have mixed up the containers. Romain and two other corporals, all equally drunk, mix up the boxes and bury a box of Guinness hidden under the French Tricolour instead of Lucien's coffin. There is no time to fix their mistake, and so the military honours are given to a case of beer.

- **Humour as a weapon**. Finally, Gary also uses humour to denounce what he disapproves of, for example, psychoanalysis:

"At the risk of shocking and disappointing some of my readers, and being perhaps regarded as an unnatural son by the fervent disciples of the great Freud: I have never had any incestuous leanings toward my mother. I also hasten to assure them that even a barbarian like myself regards the Oedipus complex with the greatest admiration and respect; I consider that its discovery does high honour to our Western civilization, and should encourage us to go on digging for the benefit of all; with the recent finding of oil in the Sahara, one of the most fruitful explorations of our underground resources."

AN EPIC NOVEL

The author describes wicked gods,: Totoche (Stupidity), Filoche (Mediocrity, Prejudice and Hatred) and Merzavka (Absolute Truth). These are epic, parodic elements which aim to thwart man's pursuit of dignity, love and justice.

Promise at Dawn is therefore also the story of Romain's fight against these gods: "I wanted to fight these absurd gods, drunk on their own power, for possession of the world, and give back the Earth to those courageous, love-filled souls who call it their home."[5] He takes up man's eternal fight against the gods for ownership of the earth and borrows certain images directly from epic tales: "I have only to raise my eyes to see the glitter of their armor in the sky, and their lances aimed at me in every beam of light", an image of a celestial battle, with hordes of divine armies marching down from the sky. The gods show their faces when he is refused

---

5. This quotation has been translated by BrightSummaries.com.

the position of non-commissioned officer out of racism, and also at several points throughout the war. This mythical backdrop helps him to remain focused on the essential fight for humanity's values by refusing to give historical events too much importance. In this way, the narration calls to mind the *Iliad*.

Gary turns his struggle against human stupidity into a myth because he refuses to blame just one race, religion or nation. In other words, he makes man's failings into an allegory, because he does not want to give a precise face to his persecutors. He could have focused on the anti-Semitism he and his mother were subjected to in Lithuania and Poland, but he decided to make a story which everyone could identify with. Wicked deities are not exclusive to Nazi Germany or the Russian and Polish pogroms: they are universal. Every victim of injustice can identify with this fight. Gary's story is no more than one part of the battle of the human soul. His "I" encompasses the whole of humanity.

THE EPIC

The epic, or epic poem, is a poetic story which tells of the mythical adventures of a hero and often includes fantastical elements. The *Iliad* and the *Odyssey*, written by the Greek poet Homer (8th century BC) are two famous examples of the genre.

THE IDEALISATION OF FRANCE

The image of France in this novel is ambiguous and unstable. Romain's mother idealises the country to the point of mythologising it. She makes it out to be a sort of El Dorado, a place where injustice does not exist and she and her son can have a better life.

This idealisation could be endangered by the many times that Romain and his mother are victims of injustice on French soil. For example, the day after their arrival, Mina tries to sell her Russian silverware and is greeted with a hostile reception by the locals, who treat her like a foreigner. Romain is also disappointed when he is not made an officer because he has only been a French citizen for a short amount of time. In spite of these failures, France seems to preserve its mythologised image, at least in the eyes of Romain's mother.

As for Romain, his impression of the country changes throughout the story. For a long time, he seems to have a very naïve view of France, thanks to everything his mother tells him about it. Several passages express his loyalty to this myth: "I have never entirely succeeded in ridding myself of that image of France seen as a nevernever land of shining heroes and exemplary virtues." During the war, he has a dogged attitude to the defence of his country, which wins him much glory in the Resistance. He wants to go off to war more than anything else, and his defence of France speaks volumes about his patriotism for his adoptive country.

However, his search for the truth and his aversion to prejudices and stereotypes influence his opinion of France. Indeed, his descriptions of the country sway between absolute admiration and a certain lucidity which, on several occasions, overcomes his love for the country:

> "It goes without saying that the day came when that highly imaginary and theoretical vision of France as seen from the depth of a Lithuanian forest collided violently with the tumultuous and contradictory reality of my country."

As a result, in spite of everything, a gap forms between his mother's idealised vision of France and the country which he sees with his own eyes, to the extent that he says that he sometimes has the impression of having never truly known the country:

> "To this day there are moments when I find myself waiting for France, for that never-never land of which I heard so much, which I have never known and never shall know; for the land of France, which from my earliest childhood, my mother conjured up for me in her lyrical and inspired descriptions, has become for me a fairy tale, a mythical place, a poetical masterpiece that no fact of life, no contact with reality could ever encompass or reveal."

This perception of France therefore puts Romain's psychological characteristics in conflict: his loyalty and his love for his mother, as well as his thirst for the truth and justice. A certain ambivalence between his naivety (which he is aware of) and his lucidity forms around this motif.

This idealisation puts several of Romain's psychological traits into perspective and is therefore fundamental in understanding the complexity of the character: with his overactive imagination, his keen view of the world, his tendency to interpret his environment with irony and his devotion to his mother, the author of *Promise at Dawn* offers us a rich, nuanced autobiographical story.

FURTHER REFLECTION

SOME QUESTIONS TO THINK ABOUT...

- Childhood dreams are very important to Gary. Why?
- What similarities can you see between *The Words*, Jean-Paul Sartre's (French philosopher and writer, 1905-1980) autobiography, and *Promise at Dawn*?
- In his Nobel Prize Banquet Speech, Albert Camus (French writer, 1913-1960) touched on a theme which is very dear to Gary. Which theme was it?
- Why can we say that *Antimemories* by André Malraux (French writer and politician, 1901-1976) is a text in a similar vein to Gary's vision? Explain your answer in detail.
- Analyse the lyricism of the cucumber in *Promise at Dawn*.
- *Promise of Dawn* has a dual meaning. What is it?
- Gary's writing presents a cult of womanhood which is rejected by feminists. Why, in your opinion?
- In what way is this an atypical autobiography?
- What makes this novel similar to an epic?
- How can literature be defined as a form of fraternity?

We want to hear from you!
Leave a comment on your online library
and share your favourite books on social media!

FURTHER READING

REFERENCE EDITION

- Gary, R. (1988) *Promise at Dawn*. Trans. Beach, J. M. Brussels: New Directions.

REFERENCE STUDY

- Schoolcraft, R. (2002) *Romain Gary: The Man Who Sold His Shadow*. Philadelphia: University of Pennsylvania Press.

ADAPTATION

- *Promise at Dawn* (1970) [Film]. Jules Dassin, dir. United States: Nathalie Productions.

MORE FROM BRIGHTSUMMARIES.COM

- Reading guide – *The Life Before Us* by Romain Gary.